Messa

IF YOU LOVE,
IT MEANS YOU ARE ALIVE!

Tatyana N. Mickushina

UDC 141.339=111=03.161.1
BBC 87.7+86.4

M59 Mickushina, T.N.
If you love, it means you are alive!
The Teaching of the Masters of Wisdom through T. N. Mickushina, 2019 – 114 pages color illustrated

In the years 2005 - 2018, T. N. Mickushina received, with the help of a special technique, Messages from the Masters of Wisdom. This comprehensive and harmonious Teaching deals with all spheres of life of humankind. In this book, different Masters present the Messages, and fragments of Messages revealing the general theme - the theme of Love.

UDC 141.339
BBC 87.7+86.4

ISBN: 9781795352048

Contents

Love, the quality of Love, true Love, the Divine Love is catastrophically lacking in your world now.

…Worlds are created by Love, and worlds collapse due to the lack of the quality of Love. It is time you should think about Love and its manifestations in your life in real earnest.

Paul the Venetian,
May 12, 2005

Preface

Throughout 2005 – 2018, I was fortunate enough to receive the Teaching in the form of Messages from the etheric octaves of Light. Over 50 Beings of Light came to give instructions and training to humanity of Earth. They are known in the different ways: The Masters of Wisdom, The Lords of Shambhala, The Great White Brotherhood, and The Ascended Masters. Among them are well-known names like: Jesus, Gautama Buddha, Lord Shiva, Mother Mary, Confucius, Zarathustra, and also the lesser well-known: The Presence of Unconditional Love, Elohim Hercules, Elohim Peace, Beloved Alpha, Lord Surya, Pallas Athena, Quan Yin and others.

The Teaching given by Them covers all the spheres of human life and is not a new Teaching. This Teaching has existed throughout the development of mankind. The language changed, the countries changed, the Messengers, through whom the Teaching was previously given, came and went, but the essence of the Teaching has remained the same, since it comes from one Divine Source.

The Teaching given through me was published in the Words of Wisdom series[1], and on the "Sirius" website[2].

We can also see certain aspects of this Teaching by collecting separate Messages on specific topics.

In this book, different Masters present the Messages, and fragments of Messages of different Beings of Light, reveal a general theme - the theme of Love.

"Love is the most essential of all the Divine qualities.

Whole worlds are created by Love. And if you do not feel joyfulness in your life, if you are weighed down by heavy thoughts and feelings, you are simply lacking Love within your being.

It does not matter whether you are loved or not. Love is a power that lives deep inside of you. And it is always with you as long as you receive the Divine Energy from its Source.

That is why a mere deficiency of this feeling of Love brings you into a discordant state of consciousness. The quality of Love runs through all of Creation and is inherently involved in your life and the lives of all living creatures.

[1] Words of Wisdom - The Teaching of the Masters of Wisdom through T. N. Mickushina. In 5 volumes – CreateSpace Independent Publishing Platform – 2017.

[2] Sirius. /Electronic resource/ Dictations, given by the Ascended Masters through the Messenger, Tatyana Mickushina - https://sirius-eng.net/dictations/mart_iun_2005/index.htm

Many of the problems in the world, if not to say all the problems of the world are directly connected with this deficiency of Love."

Djwal Kul, April 18, 2005

Divine Love and earthly love. What is the difference between them?

Is sex love? Is it so harmless to blur the moral standards that are present in our society? How can someone become a source of a beautiful feeling?

The readers will find the answers to these and many other questions when they get acquainted with the Words of Wisdom presented in this book.

Tatyana Mickushina.
Light and Love!

I encourage you to experience more often the feeling of Love for all the living. It is only Love that is capable of performing miracles in your life and in the lives of the people surrounding you.

You love, it means you are alive! And this is the most important thing.

Djwal Kul,
April 18, 2005

Open your hearts to Divine Love
and you will change this world

The Presence of
Unconditional Love
March 7, 2005

The Presence of Unconditional Love
March 7, 2005

...The quality of Love is the greatest of all the Divine qualities. The aspiration to love, the desire to love and to be loved is characteristic of all living creatures. It is due however to the breach of the Divine Law, which happened through the misuse of free will in the times of ancient Lemuria and Atlantis that the greatest distortions were brought into this quality.

If we manage to completely restore this quality in the souls of just a few people embodied now, we could disseminate it around the world very quickly. And this quality of Divine Love is impossible to oppose.

This is the quality that allows you to tune into the Divine Reality immediately.

Very often this quality is mixed up with the sexual instinct. Hence, different sexual perversions take place.

The ability of man to do creative work, his creative power is manifested through Love. The creative power that is the basis in the conception of a child, is at the same time the basis of everything created by man in his life.

Man is inherently similar to God. The keynote quality of God is Love. Thus, it is impossible for Man not to create.

But the creative power can be manifested only in as much as it is not limited by blocks of anti-love imbedded into man's consciousness from outside, and supported by his imperfect consciousness from within.

The Perfect Flame of Love comes to this world through your I AM Presence. But the filters of your imperfect thoughts and feelings are in the path of this stream of Love. As a result, the stream is distorted. You are constantly manifesting the quality of Divine Love. It is impossible for you not to manifest this quality, as it is inherent in all creation. But you should simply purge the filters from both your consciousness, and your perception of the Divine Reality.

Open your hearts to Love, Divine Love, and you will change this world.

There is no force mightier than Love in this world.

Therefore, those forces that have decided to separate from God live off the distortions of the quality of Divine Love.

The entire industry of sex and pornography, stereotypes of interrelations between the sexes, propagandized and circulated by mass media is aimed precisely at keeping you from any manifestation of Divine Love.

It seems harmless if you watch a film cultivating your desire to satisfy your sexual instinct. It seems to be an innocent amusement to look at a naked female body, advertising objects that are absolutely unnecessary for your spiritual development.

As a result, hatred for Divine Love settles in your consciousness. You voluntarily strengthen the filters that are embedded in your consciousness, and are preventing you from manifesting the quality of true Love in your life.

It is impossible to draw a comparison, but there is a huge difference between the primordial Divine manifestation of Love, and the understanding of love that has settled into people's consciousness since the days of the fallen civilizations.

It is like life and death.

One of the qualities of the saints is their ability to absorb the nectar of Divine Grace into their hearts. There is no pleasure in this physical world that can be compared to receiving this Divine Grace.

Only pure hearts are capable of obtaining this Grace.

A stream of the Divine energy and Divine Love passes through all your bodies and caresses you. You experience ecstasy in every chakra, every energetic center.

The greatest sexual satisfaction that you can have in the physical life cannot be compared with the experience of Grace sent to you by God.

Think whether it is harmless for you to watch pornographic films, to tolerate foul language, to be in the company of people allowing dirty thoughts and actions in their attitude toward women and sexual interrelations.

Each of these negative vibrations contributes to your separation from the quality of Divine Love.

Contemplate flowers, nature, and children's smiles. Constantly guard your love against any manifestation of anti-love. Guard your relatives and your children. The future of your planet depends on the conception of Love that will be obtained by the new generation.

True Love begins with the veneration of a woman, a Mother. The feelings you experience towards your Mother can leave their mark on your whole life. The happiest families are those where the respect for the Mother as the keeper of the hearth, has become a tradition.

May your consciousness never be burdened by any bad thoughts directed against the Mother, against the female Source.

All of you are mothers in this world, both men and women. You have descended into your embodiments to master the quality of the Divine Mother. Therefore, your correct attitude toward a woman, a Mother is a guarantee of your successful acquirement of the quality of the Divine Mother. Without mastering this quality, you will not be able to know the Father and the Son.

I wish you to acquire the quality of Divine Love in your present embodiment.

I AM the Presence of Unconditional Love, and I caress you with the rays of my Love.

Cultivate the feeling of Love
in your heart

Beloved Djwal Kul
April 18, 2005

Beloved Djwal Kul
April 18, 2005

I AM Djwal Kul, having come on the ray of Love through this Messenger.

Yes, beloved, I AM, having come to you today to affirm Love.

Love is the most essential of all the Divine qualities.

Whole worlds are created by Love. And if you do not feel joyfulness in your life, if you are weighed down by heavy thoughts and feelings, you are simply lacking Love within your being.

It does not matter whether you are loved or not. Love is a power that lives deep inside of you. And it is always with you as long as you receive the Divine Energy from its Source.

That is why a mere deficiency of this feeling of Love brings you into a discordant state of consciousness. The quality of Love runs through all of Creation and is inherently involved in your life and the lives of all living creatures.

Many of the problems in the world, if not to say all the problems of the world are directly connected with this deficiency of Love.

I have come to give you advice on how to anchor the focus of Love within your heart.

Promise me that you will perform this exercise every day whenever you have a free minute. This exercise requires neither special preparation nor additional conditions. You may perform this exercise at home or at work, even among people in the busiest places.

Thus, you should always see in your mind's eye the image of a person you love. I understand very well that many of you may say that you do not feel love towards anybody in this world. This is a delusion. You must love. You must find in your consciousness an image towards which you feel love.

I do not mean by this that it must be an image of your beloved. But search in the depth of your heart attentively and try to find that image towards which you are able to feel love.

This can be your mother, your father, your spouse, or your children. This can be an Ascended Master with whom you have an inner link.

If your heart suffers from a trauma so severe that the very reminder of your beloved causes self-pity and tears in your eyes, you should still look for an image towards which you could aspire with your consciousness, and towards which you could feel Love.

It could even be your pet or favorite plants.

Cultivate the feeling of Love in your heart.

Your foremost task in life is to regain the feeling of Love at any price.

If you are surrounded by people, try to feel love towards the people around you. Love people not for something they have done, or can do for you; just feel Love that is unconditional.

Maybe you will not be able to concentrate on your feeling of Love for long. But you should find at least two or three minutes a day to experience this feeling of Love.

Cultivate this feeling inside of you.

And the day will come when you will be able to experience a strong, all-consuming and causeless feeling of Love for everything surrounding you, for all people living on Earth, for the very Earth, for nature, clouds, sky, rain, sun.

You will be overwhelmed with the feeling of Love and Oneness with everything surrounding you. But you are all this simultaneously. Understand that your consciousness, your human consciousness separates you from everything surrounding you, but your real nature and the nature of everything around you are the same.

All is God. And your separation from the Oneness with God is only in your consciousness.

Let's talk about something else. I want to make use of this opportunity in order to give you certain knowledge or information that will be valuable for you exactly at this period of time.

You have been embodied on Earth at this difficult time when a division is taking place in your world. Space cycles have changed, and new energies have come to Earth — the energies of Love and Unity. These energies are being brought to Earth due to the influence of planet Venus, which is my native planet.

There is no living creature in the world that does not experience the influence of these energies.

However, these energies do not have a beneficial influence on all people. In your world, there are beings that have broken their link with the Divine Source so much that their being is already unable to perceive these energies. They are dead. Just as the sun shines on all plants and exerts a beneficial influence upon them helping them to develop and to be active, in the same way the sun also shines on withered plants that are already dead. But under the sun's influence, these plants fade even more and become fit only for stoking stoves.

That is why everything moribund will soon be collected and burned in the cosmic furnace.

A good gardener keeps an eye on his garden and burns withered trees, preventing mold from spreading onto healthy plants.

The words I am telling you now are very sad. But it is the truth you face in life. Losses are inevitable and each of you chooses his own path by himself. You make a choice every minute of your time on Earth. You make a choice either in favor of God and Life, or you choose death. You have heard so many times that the time to separate the grain from the weeds is approaching. You have heard many times that the weeds must be separated and burned.

Not even those who are very far from God can say they have not heard this phrase at least once in their life.

Then what are you wondering about? The time has come. Those people who cannot assimilate the new vibrations, and are not able to transition to the new level of consciousness will find themselves in the hands of the gardener, who will care only about their further plight.

And the gardener of our Universe is God Himself.

That is why you have nothing to worry about. Everything takes place due to God's Will and all the deadlines and the work connected with these deadlines will be observed on time and in strict accordance with God's plan. What are you to do at this time? Learn from nature. Go out to the woods and look at the things happening there.

There are dried up trees and decomposing stumps. But there are young sprouts as well. And life goes on. Bees buzz, birds sing, flowers are in full bloom. Harmony reigns there in all its richness. Each of you is a unique flower in these woods. Thus, you should be in full bloom and feel Love towards everything around you.

Follow nature's example. A flower simply blooms. It fights neither with dried up trees nor with a decomposing stump. Everything submits to the Divine Law and everything takes place in accordance with the Divine Law.

Believe me, there are such servants in the Universe whose job is to cleanse the Universe from impurities, and from everything that is dead, or does not wish to observe the established Law.

You have heard about the time for the harvest. You thought that the harvest time was drawing near, but due to various reasons, none of you were concerned when the time for reaping came. Now an extensive reaping is taking place.

Everything takes place so naturally that people do not even notice this reaping. Everything takes place according to the terms fixed by and in full accordance with the Higher Law.

I have given you much valuable information today. And regardless of the fact that this information has been given by me in a very soft manner, many of you will still be sad to hear about the events happening on Earth now.

Nevertheless, I still encourage you to experience more often the feeling of Love for all the living. It is only Love that is capable of performing miracles in your life and in the lives of the people surrounding you.

You love and it means you are alive! And this is the most important thing.

**I AM Djwal Kul,
and I have been with you today.**

A Teaching on the energy of the Divine Mother

Beloved Paul the Venetian
May 12, 2005

Beloved Paul the Venetian
May 12, 2005

I AM Paul the Venetian, having come to you.

I AM the Chohan[3] of the Third Ray, the Ray of Love. You can hardly find so many distortions on the other rays as we meet on the Ray of Love on Earth. And it is quite explainable. If all the other Divine qualities were distorted by the dual state of the world but only the quality of Divine Love was preserved in its primordial shape, the whole world would have another appearance. Love, the quality of Love, true Love, Divine Love is catastrophically lacking in your world now.

I have come to affirm Love. I have come to impart Love to you.

Worlds are created by Love, and worlds collapse due to the lack of the quality of Love. It is time you should think about Love and its manifestations in your life in real earnest.

In reality, the heart chakra which passes the energies of Love into your physical world, is completely blocked in the majority of people. Therefore, you feel a lack of Love, and you try to compensate for its shortage

---

[3] Chohan is a term meaning lord or master. It is a title of respect and honor, and a specific Chohan presides over each of the seven rays. These seven Chohans, or Lords of the Rays, have specialized in applying the qualities of their ray throughout their many incarnations on Earth, and they can instruct us in how to gain self-mastery on that ray. (Translator's footnote.)

by strange practices stimulating a purely physiological instinct. Trust me, the majority of distortions of the Divine Energy in your world are connected exactly with the misuse of the energy of the Divine Mother or, in other words, your sexual energy.

God endowed you with the Sacred Fire, the Flame of the Sacred Fire, which makes you similar to Gods. And believe me, this flame and this energy are not given to you so you can use them for your pleasure. The more thoughtlessly you use your Sacred Fire, the more karma you create. Your mass media and the stereotypes of behavior in your society, even your way of behaving and dressing, stimulate the misuse of your sexual energy.

In the course of time you will be able to understand the true purpose of the gift of the Sacred Fire granted to you by God. But now you ought to understand that every time you use this gift not in accordance with the Divine purpose, you create karma. You create karma because you waste the Divine Energy to receive empty, purely animal pleasures. However, animals act much more reasonably than you in this respect. Their use of sexual energy happens at least in the framework of yearly cycles at an appropriate time of the year.

During the act of sexual intercourse, a gigantic amount of Divine Energy is released. This release of Divine Energy can be compared with the flash of a supernova. And you know that your energy flows in exactly the same direction as your attention. And if at the moment of release of the Divine Energy, you think of receiving pleasure for yourself and your partner, you use your sexual energy for the wrong purpose. Many of you may find my words impossible to absorb into your consciousness. I am absolutely aware that my words will sound strange to many of you. But I must inform you about the very elementary foundations of the Divine Ethics, with which even animals are familiar, but which for some reason humanity has forgotten.

Everything in this world belongs to God. You are particles of God. Therefore, everything you do, all your actions must conform to the Divine Law and take place within the framework of this Law. If you do something against the Will of God, you violate the Law of this Universe and create karma. Thus, no matter how strange my instructions and recommendations seem to you, please at least just listen to them first.

Before an act of sexual intercourse, please make sure your actions are in-tune with the Will of God. You must be in lawful wedlock with your sexual partner. You should not engage in any sexual relationship with casual partners and with people of the same sex as you.

Why is it so necessary to be in lawful wedlock with a constant partner?

The point is that while performing your marital duty there is a direct exchange of energy between you and your partner. During regular communication with people you constantly exchange energies, but your energy exchange during sexual intercourse is greatly multiplied. In fact, you exchange all your energies — both good and bad. You take upon yourselves each other's karma, and you share your merits with your sexual partners. If you are in lawful wedlock, then during your mutual life you have an opportunity to work off not only your own karma but also the karma of your spouse, if your spouse's karma outweighs yours.

Now imagine that you have a sexual relationship with many partners. And imagine that the percent of the karma they have worked off is much less than yours. Their karmic debts can be much heavier than yours. Perhaps they came to this world to work off the karma of murder, betrayal, or some other dire kinds of karma. So when you absolutely thoughtlessly enter into a sexual relationship with them, you take upon yourself a part of their karma. And if at the same time you are in lawful wedlock, you take this karma upon your family. And after that you wonder why you have all your life problems?

Sexual energy has the same nature as the energy used for creativity, creation in your world. And when you waste your sexual potential for pleasure, you deprive yourself of creative energy and limit your evolution. In reality, the majority of the population has been so devastated by the abuse of sexual energy that when they approach maturity they are absolutely unable to perform higher creative activity. They are simply incapable of becoming co-creators with God, or even performing the usual creative work for your world.

The purpose of my Dictation today is to raise a very important question before you. I am doing it as openly and as frankly as possible, because I repeat again, that it is exactly through the abuse of the energy of the Divine Mother that the greatest part of energy is distorted by mankind.

Every act of intercourse within wedlock should be performed in the name of God. Pray to God and dedicate the Sacred Fire that will be released during your sexual intercourse to God. Remember that your energy flows in exactly the same direction as your attention. And if you, during the release of your Sacred Fire, dedicate this release to God, you will direct all the freed energy into the higher realms of Light. And this energy will return to you afterwards as blessings for you and your children.

Try to use the Energy of the Divine Mother only for conceiving children. If you initially find it difficult to take on such restrictions, then try to cut down the number of your acts of intercourse to once or twice a week. Do not forget to, at least mentally, direct all the energy released to God. Ask God to use this energy for blessing you, your children, and your whole family.

Always remember that all your actions in the physical plane can be used both for good or for evil. Every minute and every second of your life in the physical world, you receive the Divine Energy, and you either direct it for the creation of the illusion — where it forms a sediment in this world and multiplies the illusion— or you direct your energy towards the Divine world, creating good karma and multiplying your merits and treasures in Heaven.

The use of your sexual energy should be the cornerstone of your life.

I would like you to thoroughly familiarize yourselves with my lecture today and to try to apply all my recommendations in your life.

I AM Paul the Venetian.

You Love.

No matter how hard you hide your Love or pretend that you do not remember your Love, it is present within you all the same.

Your basic quality is Love.

Remove all unnecessary things from your life that prevent you from feeling the Divine Love in your heart.

Beloved Alpha
January 6, 2006

A Teaching
on Love

Lord Maitreya
May 27, 2005

Lord Maitreya
May 27, 2005

I AM Lord Maitreya, having come again through this Messenger!

The charm of our contact and the information that I am going to share will be of use to you.

It is so seldom that we have an opportunity to commune with the non-ascended mankind. And you are given an opportunity to be in touch with the Ascended Hosts so rarely that there cannot be any superfluous information, and the time that you spend while reading this Dictation will be delightful.

I would like to speak to you about the most essential matter. I wish to have a word on this topic because there is nothing more important for you now.

If a miracle occurred and all the people began to experience the feeling of Love, I can assure you that an instantaneous miracle of transformation would happen. Love is the quality that your world is constantly lacking. However, in reality Love is the quality that is inherent in this world primordially. Your constant feeling of the shortage of Love is evidence that you are following a wrong Path.

If only you could continually experience this beautiful all-embracing feeling! In this case, your mind and your emotional body could be in an elevated state all the time, and you would be able to keep your vibrations continually on the highest level available for you.

What else do you need beloved?

When a man becomes filled with high vibrations, when he is full of the feeling of Divine Love, he feels a causeless state of happiness, and his life becomes full of the sense of peace, and harmony.

I do not mean the quality that is called love by the majority of humans on Earth, and that in fact, has nothing in common with the true Love, pure Love — Divine Love.

I can tell you with a feeling of full certainty and trustworthiness that the true feeling of Love is as big a rarity in your world as your meeting with the Ascended Hosts.

If you were able to raise your vibrations up to the feeling of Divine Love for at least a very short time, you would manage to commune with the Ascended Hosts almost instantaneously.

The Ascended Hosts are very responsive to the quality of Love. That is why we ask you to send us your Love. There is no greater happiness for us than to feel your Love.

And if you are vibrating at the frequency of Love, you can also feel our Love the same way.

In many Teachings, given through many Messengers, it was said that Love is a key. Do you understand now why Love is a key?

It is because this feeling is able to raise your vibrations instantaneously and to approximate them to the vibrations of the etheric octaves of Light. And you become able to come into contact with any Master towards whom you experience the feeling of Divine Love at a given moment.

This feeling of Love, true Love, Divine Love, when being experienced by you, is a signal of your readiness to communicate with our world. This very feeling of Love creates for you an absolutely impenetrable defense from the attacks of any negative forces and energies, and of any individuals who have submitted themselves to the actions of these forces.

That is why it is very easy to identify the direction of your movement. If you experience a feeling of causeless Love, joy, and peace, then you are moving in the right direction. You are ready to embrace the entire world and you are ready to give help to the whole world.

You are seized by causeless generosity, happiness, and a wish to give out more and more of your Light and your Love, to grant your Love to the world and to ask nothing in exchange.

On the contrary, if you have lost your way and are going in the wrong direction, you feel a deficiency of Love and, as a consequence of this, suspiciousness, fear, and condemnation. Any person filled with Love will differ so much from you by his vibrations that you will feel irritation towards him.

You see that the criterion of the faultlessness of the Path that you follow is very simple.

You either experience the feeling of Love or you do not have it.

And since only a very small percent of the people of Earth can feel this noble feeling, you can judge how many people are moving on the right Path…

I AM Maitreya, with Love towards you.

There are no barriers
for
the power of Love

Beloved Mother Mary
June 13, 2005

Beloved Mother Mary
June 13, 2005

...I am happy to meet you today... And I thank all of you who have devoted all your free time to saying Rosaries...

...My Love was invariably being poured upon you during your saying of the Rosaries. And I was feeling your Love. Oh, you cannot even imagine the bliss I experience while taking your Love into my heart. Your Love penetrates the veil and flows like blessed incense wrapping me. I always see clearly whose heart is sending me this Love, and I can always send my blessing to your heart, to your life-stream.

Blessed be all those devoted and compassionate hearts who, amid the hustle and bustle of the day, find time to stop and give me Love and the energy of the Rosary. Let us not interrupt this flow of Love and this energy exchange between our octaves.

Just imagine that each of your prayers addressed to me makes the veil between our worlds thinner and thinner. There are regions on the globe where the power of your prayers has made the communication between our worlds possible to such an extent that you can even feel me touching you and sense the aroma of the roses I am heaping upon you.

Beloved, do not interrupt your prayers.

I need your Love and prayers as before...

...Do you remember Serafim Sarovsky? Can you remember him serving before my image on the icon called Tenderness? He did not even recite prayers, but his eyes filled with tears, and he plunged into a totally blissful state of Love towards me. Serafim Sarovsky was one of my most devoted servants. And I still remember the moments of our commune spent together in the woods.

You cannot even imagine this inexpressible miracle given to us by the Lord. With the help of our Love we are able to eliminate all the barriers between our worlds. And there is nothing more elevated, pleasant and blessed than the communication that we can give each other.

We exist on different sides of the border separating our worlds. However, the border itself is becoming thinner and thinner under the influence of the overmastering power of Love. There are no barriers for the power of Love, beloved.

Love is capable of working miracles both in your world and ours. And Love is the very force capable of penetrating the veil.

When you have a minute to leave your bustle and go before my image, please do not think that I am somewhere far away. I hear the sincere call of your heart. I am where you are. I hear every word you say to me, no matter whether you pronounce these words aloud or just within your heart.

And if you bate your breath and look narrowly, you can even spot my presence next to you in the shape of a light, subtle cloud. You can also sense a dainty aroma of the roses or feel me touching you.

I love watching your faces during your prayers. And sometimes I allow myself to approach you while you are saying the Rosaries and to kiss or stroke you.

You, many of you, feel my touches and even try to drive me away like an annoying fly. Oh, if you only admitted in your consciousness a thought that it was not a fly but Mother Mary herself who came to kiss you. You would feel very awkward and funny.

Our worlds are much closer to each other than you can imagine. And even now, you can feel my presence during your prayers. There is no closer Master than me for the people of Earth. I answer literally all your requests. And I am very sorry that at times your karma is so heavy that I cannot give you the help you ask me for. However, nothing is impossible for God. And after you have realized your past mistakes at the new level, it is possible that I will be allowed to help you…

…Meanwhile, I ask you not to stop the wheel of prayers. And if due to your stirring life you cannot dedicate much time to prayers, I think you can always find time and a chance, amid the bustle of the day to cast a look at my image or an icon and give me your Love.

It will take mere seconds. But if you are able to send me your Love just a few times during a day, this will substitute for the reading of Rosaries and prayers.

Always have my image with you. Keep my image in your handbag or in an amulet. Always remember that there in the physical world where my focus is, I can establish my presence owing to the energy of Love that you send me.

Please be patient, beloved. It is not too long to wait. Come out at dawn and feel the delightful moment when the Sun is still below the horizon, but everybody around is already anticipating this instant of the sunrise. And right now the whole world is at this point of expecting the rise of the Sun — the Sun of Faith, the Sun of Love, and the Sun of Hope.

The sunrise of your consciousness is as inevitable as the rise of the Sun foreseen by your being.

I AM Mother Mary, always loving you and waiting for our meeting.

Accept
my Fatherly
Love

Beloved Alpha
January 6, 2006

Beloved Alpha
January 6, 2006

…Listen to the call of your heart.

Stay alone in silence and listen to what your heart is whispering to you.

You can't help hearing this. Remove all unnecessary things from your life, everything that does not give you an opportunity to stay alone and listen to the voice of your heart, to hear its tender whisper, and to feel its Love.

You Love. No matter how hard you hide your Love or pretend that you do not remember your Love, it is present within you all the same. Your basic quality is Love. Remove all unnecessary things from your life that prevent you from feeling the Divine Love in your heart.

You choose on your own, and you create all the circumstances of your life.

Haven't you gotten tired of giving in to those stereotypes and habits that envelop you? Hasn't the time come to give up all the fuss around you and turn with all your being to the Eternal, the everlasting?

I have come in order to remind you once again of that place from which your souls have come into this world. I have come to remind you once again of your Home and call you Home.

Can you hear me? Oh, my children.

I am ready to render all the care of my Fatherly heart to you. I am ready to give you the Love of my heart again and again. I just need your decision, your firm decision that you will make in your heart, and will never walk away from the chosen decision anymore. And that decision is to return Home and to complete everything that is necessary in order to come back Home, to your Fatherly Home that you left and where you are to return.

All of you represent the particles of the One. Your separation and wandering in your cold and uncomfortable world are coming to an end. All of you will return Home. I am waiting. I am looking forward to seeing each of you, my beloved but not always obedient children.

Accept my Fatherly Love.

I am sending the gift of my Love to each of you, straight from my heart to your hearts.

Hold up the chalice of your heart, and I shall fill it with my Love up to the brim!

When it gets hard for you in your world, you will remember my Love. You will be able to say a prayer-call, and I shall come to cover you with my Love and help you overcome your troubles and misfortunes, and help you go through the most difficult part of the Path.

To do that you should simply say in your heart: "Father, I'm Yours. Come, help me."

And I will come at the most difficult moment of your tests.

I cannot leave you in trouble, and I cannot help Loving you — each of you... with my Love — with the Love that does not require anything in return.

I AM Alpha, your Heavenly Father.

The success of your
evolution on your
beautiful planet
depends on the
development of the
quality of Divine Love
in you

Beloved Surya
July 4, 2006

Beloved Surya
July 4, 2006

I AM Surya, having come to you today. I AM, having come to you from the Great Central Sun to open another page of the eternal Teaching about Eternal Life and the absence of death. It may seem to you that I am using a very pompous language; however, it is the usual language in the circles and octaves where I come from. Our language does not resemble yours. We speak the language of thought, and not even so much the language of thought as the language of energy. We exchange energies, and it is similar to your exchanging your feelings of Love. I have just told you one of the greatest secrets of Space. Everything in this universe is based on the great power of Love, and everything that there is in this universe exists only due to the power of Love.

Love is the essence of this universe. Therefore, your vibrations are solely the vibrations of Love when they are as close to the vibrations of the universe as possible. The more you are able to manifest the quality of Love in your heart, the closer you get to the true reality and move away from your physical illusion. However, there is a big difference between the shades of the quality of Love in your world and in ours. What many of you mean by Love, is in fact not Love at all. That feeling which you sometimes call love is equal to the sexual instinct, or the instinct of a sex, and there is no difference between that feeling and the one which birds or animals have. Therefore, first of all, you should think about the quality of the Love you experience. True Love has no attachment at all to a definite sex or to the object of Love. This is an inner feeling, having no attachment to a definite being or an object; it is Love toward everyone, toward the whole of creation, the whole of Life, and the whole universe. Many of you, being in nature, can raise your vibrations to that true feeling of Love. But the power and the fullness of that Love can be even more intense. Your physical bodies simply cannot experience more elevated and more subtle manifestations of this amazing quality of Love. Each of you shows love in your own way, and each of you has your own inherent individual and personal understanding of the quality of Love. At the beginning of Creation, God divided his Love into an infinite number of parts, and each of you, being a part of God, received your own little part of Love. Now you have an opportunity to experience that Love and to refine it. That is why you have to get rid of everything in your life that prevents your feeling of Love from growing within you. Observe your lives thoroughly, and try to trace the states you experience most often. You will be surprised that you hardly ever experience the feeling of Love that is inherent in the whole of Creation, the true feeling of Love. And even when the time of your first love comes, it is very seldom that this feeling is not colored with a possessive instinct and the desire to own the object of your love. Therefore, the success of your evolution on your beautiful planet depends on the development of the quality of Divine Love in you.

That is why I have come today to give you this Message based on the feeling of great Love toward mankind of Earth.

And if the other Ascended Masters and I didn't have that feeling of unconditional, perfect Love within, we would hardly have been able to come and babysit you, care about you, and to give our Teachings and instructions during the whole cycle of the evolution of the material universe.

We know quite well that no matter how you resist, you do not have a choice, and sooner or later, you will follow the path destined for you by the plan of the great Creator of this Universe.

And that is the path of the highest Love and the highest bliss. Everything that separates you from that state is subject to gradual refusal and must leave your consciousness and your lives, for such is the Law. You have to make your own choice and to follow this Law — the Law of the highest and unconditional Love.

Now it is hard for you to believe that everything around you is just the manifestation of the non-divine feeling of anti-love. Yes, everything you have created that is not based on the great feeling of Love will disappear in the course of time and will stop existing. What will be left is only what is perfect in God, which is primarily the feeling of Divine unconditional Love, not clouded by human consciousness.

I am very happy to give you this Teaching today. It is a pleasure to talk about Love and to feel Love for you, children of Earth. You cannot even imagine how happy I am.

Now I would like to say a few words concerning our future plans. These plans do not differ from everything you have already heard. We continue to pull mankind of Earth to the level of evolution that it must be at, but for which it is still reluctant to attain. It seems to you that you have made great achievements, but all of your achievements are directed at multiplying the illusion. But at the current stage, other achievements are required of you: the achievements in the field of developing the Divine qualities within you, with Divine Love as the main quality. However, there are other qualities that you have to develop in yourselves. In order for you to concentrate on the true inner achievements, you should turn and look inside of yourselves. This is exactly the path that we teach, the path of mystics, the path leading you to your Source.

But in order for you to follow that path, you must renounce your attachments to the world and the achievement of any kind of goals in your world. It is very difficult, because in order for you to attain an inner connection with us and with your Higher Self, you need unconditional and absolute Faith. Faith and Love are two sisters, two loving sisters who are inseparable in eternity. There is also Hope. Hope alone can unfold your consciousness when it seems to you that there is no way out of the deadlock and disorder of the storms of life.

That is why we come, in order to keep you in harmony with the Higher reality and to give you Hope for tomorrow, which will no doubt be better than today. For such is the Law of this universe. And with every successive cycle of evolution, you will get closer and closer to the Divine Reality, and it will become easier and easier for you. In the course of time, the awareness of this reality will come, and happiness will overflow in you and will never leave you. The twilight of your consciousness is coming to an end. The new dawn and the awakening in the new reality are ahead./

I am happy to announce to you the coming of the new reality, the sun of the new reality into your world.

I AM Surya, having come to you with a feeling of great Love!

Only with the feeling of unconditional, infinite Love are you able to build true relations in your world.

Beloved Jesus
December 31, 2007

Guidance
for every day

Beloved Kuthumi
June 26, 2007

Beloved Kuthumi
June 26, 2007

… Again and again we come, clarify, and give the understanding of many things that are known to you already. Yet, the facets that open up for you allow you to enjoy the new brilliance of the precious stones of the good old knowledge.

We come and you become filled with our energy and our Love again. That is because it is impossible to give the Teaching and not to Love at the same time. All knowledge and understanding come with the feeling of deep, unconditional Love. We give our knowledge based on Love, and you are able to comprehend the information that we provide only when you are able to feel deep unconditional Love for me, for other Masters, and for our Messenger.

Only based on the feelings of Divine Love are you able to comprehend the Truth. This is the law that works unalterably when the energy is being exchanged between the octaves. When you experience fear, doubt, and other imperfect feelings, you will be unable to comprehend the whole perfection of the Divine Truth. On the other hand, if you are able to cultivate this feeling of unconditional Divine Love, you will be able to see tremendous Truth, even in one single phrase. This phrase will mean nothing to the majority of mankind, but for you it will open up the whole fullness of the Divine Truth because you have received the key to open it, namely: the Divine Love in your heart. Therefore, do not strive to cultivate the pursuit of knowledge; strive to cultivate the Divine Love in yourself. Your perfection in God is not possible if you cannot develop this quality of Divine Love within yourselves.

You cannot imagine how quickly and clearly humanity will begin to advance along the Divine Path if you are able to understand the importance of the all-encompassing feeling of Love. Many, if not almost all the tests on your Path can be overcome only with the feeling of Love. When Divine Love leaves you, it can be compared to a serious illness. Nobody will help you with that illness if you do not desire to return to the elevated state of consciousness and to the feeling of all-encompassing Love. The feeling of unconditional Love is what you lack; this is what will be the best remedy for you on the spiritual Path.

It is impossible to feel Love if you are driven by other imperfect feelings — for example, the feeling of fear arises due to the shortage of Love. You are afraid of losing something or you are afraid that someone will harm you, but the reason why you have these fears is because you do not have Love in your heart. Therefore, the best remedy for fear is Love, the Love that is Divine in its essence. If you have Love that is not Divine, then that imperfect feeling can tie you to the object of your affection. You should feel unconditional Love, which is not associated with a particular person but to a more general Love. You should love every being in your world and every being in the Divine world.

When you see too many imperfections in other people, it also means that you lack Love. You cannot notice imperfections and feel Love at the same time. These are incompatible qualities.

In the beginning it will be difficult for you to experience the feeling of unconditional Love. That is because your understanding of love is much too related to human sentiments. Therefore, do not be ashamed if, in the beginning, your love is not perfect.

The strength of your Love is also important. That is because Love is the quality that allows you to act in your world. Strength without Love turns into craftiness and resentment. Therefore, you need to start and do everything in your lives only with the feeling of Love. If you have any personal motive, it makes all your actions imperfect. When you try to do a good deed only with your mind, without hearing the sound of the Divine feeling of Love within you, your deed may lead to a bad result instead of a good outcome.

Remember what Jesus taught you: "By their fruits you will recognize them."[4]

Your actions may be absolutely correct — you may be praying, doing community service, helping others — but no matter what you do, it will lead to poor results.

---

[4] By their fruit you will recognize them. (Mathew 7:16).
No good tree bears bad fruit, nor does a bad tree bear good fruit. Each tree is recognized by its own fruit. (Luke 6:43-44)

This happens because at the moment when you decided to do something, your intention was not colored with Love. Thus, the fruit, the result of your actions, turned out to be rotten. Therefore, if I were you, I would rather not do anything instead of starting something without the feeling of Love. That is because karma, as the result of your actions, will be negative in this case.

Do you understand how the Law of karma works? Do you understand that more and more subtle aspects of this Law are revealed to you as you advance on your Path? That is why we give our Teaching. For those who began reading our Messages very recently and who did not read all Dictations from the beginning but instead began reading the last cycle of the Messages, many things that we are talking about will be unclear.

Once again, I have to make the analogy of an educational institution. When you go to school, first you go to the first grade, and then you transfer to the second and third grades. Only very arrogant people can go straight to the tenth grade and demand to study there. Knowledge cannot fill a vessel if the vessel is not prepared properly. We are responsible for ensuring that you understand the Teaching that we give. That is why we teach you very complex Truths in very simple words; many people become confused by that. It seems to them that everything we say is old truths.

Allow me to note that in this case you are driven by your ego, and the lack of Divine Love will one day play an evil trick on you. That is why we give our Messages based on the feeling of deep, unconditional Love, but you also need to accept the nectar of our Teaching when you are attuned to the Divine tone and filled with Love. I do not recommend that you begin reading our Messages until you reach a balanced state of consciousness. Think about what I said, and try to find the mechanisms in your life that will help you to come into a balanced state of consciousness.

I would recommend that you pay attention to every small detail that surrounds you in your lives. You should maintain tidiness in your house and at your workplace. You should carefully select the food you eat and maintain the cleanliness of your body. Note to yourselves that in addition to physical dirt, you also collect a lot of astral and mental dirt throughout the day. The best way of cleaning yourselves from that dirt will be bathing in a pure natural reservoir or at least taking a shower or a full bath twice daily, in the morning and in the evening.

I was with you on this day to provide guidance regarding everyday life. Do not think that what has been said does not concern each of you individually.

I AM Kuthumi.

The quality of Love is the greatest of all the Divine qualities. The aspiration to love, the desire to love and to be loved is characteristic of all living creatures.

The Presence of
Unconditional Love
March 7, 2005

Instructions
for
every day

Beloved Jesus
December 31, 2007

Beloved Jesus
December 31, 2007

I AM Jesus, beloved by you. I have come to renew our relationship based on mutual love. You Love me, don't you?

I visited Earth 2000 years ago. And one of the aims and the tasks of my coming was to give the humanity of Earth an example of Love — not the Love based on the fleshly desire, but the Love based on a more elevated Divine feeling.

I spoke about it, and I taught my disciples about the relationships founded on this feeling of Love. The relationships based on the mutual feelings of Love are the only necessary condition when a community — several people or families — gather to live together.

It is difficult for you to understand this feeling that one feels toward all people without exception. However, I had this gift. God gave me this ability: to Love all people. It is thanks to this ability that I was able to withstand all the ordeals that God sent to me.

Only with the feeling of unconditional, infinite Love are you able to build true relations in your world.

You are used to feeling love for your parents, for men and women, and for children. All of these are different manifestations of one and the same Divine Love. But these are only small manifestations, narrow ones. I am telling you about greater Love, about the Love that does not differentiate men, women, children, animals, and even inanimate nature.

I am telling you about the Love that expands boundlessly and includes the whole Creation, everything that surrounds you.

It is very hard to feel such Love in your world. However, if you do not learn to Love in this way, you will not be able to move along the Path of evolutionary development that we are teaching you.

The Ascended Masters, who direct the evolutions of the planet Earth, all possess this quality of Love in varying degrees. Believe me, if we did not feel tremendous all-embracing Love toward you, we simply could not have managed to endure these millions of years, during which we have been working with the humankind of planet Earth. We feel Love toward you not because you are so good, but because you are part of God. There is an un-manifested particle of God in every one of you, and the task for each of you is to manifest God, to give God the opportunity to act through you.

Now you are too preoccupied and anxious about your worldly affairs. You are constantly in a hurry, and you are toiling over the fulfillment of large and small tasks of life. The time will come when you will be able to discern a more global picture of the development of human civilization behind the whole fuss of life. You will learn to watch and see how every life situation that arises before your sight has causes that come into action from what you yourselves have created earlier. You will learn to distinguish causes from effects. Gradually you will be able to unravel the tapestry of Life and to see the reality that exists behind it. You will be able to discern the real world of God.

For now, you have much to learn, and more that you have yet to understand…

**I AM Jesus,
your brother and helper on the Path.**

Love is the essence of this universe. Therefore, your vibrations are solely the vibrations of Love when they are as close to the vibrations of the universe as possible.

Beloved Surya
July 4, 2006

The internal
and external
Teaching

Beloved Jesus
June 25, 2008

Beloved Jesus
June 25, 2008

… Never chase external rituals. Never try to find sacraments where there are none. Live simply. Follow the commandments given by Moses and the prophets, and first and foremost, try to maintain in your heart the feeling of Love and compassion toward your neighbor, and all living beings.

The way you treat every particle of Life, the way you treat any Divine manifestation will distinguish a true believer from a hypocrite who covers up with the name of God, but does not have God in his heart.

I gave you the commandment "Love each other". I have come in order to tell you that when Love lives in your heart, you do not need any external preacher; you do not need to spend your time searching for God outside of yourselves, because you have Love and therefore, you reside in God because God is Love.

I have come to you today in order to give you understanding of the internal Teaching that resides in your hearts and that is Love.

I AM Jesus.

Man is inherently similar to God. The keynote quality of God is Love. Thus, it is impossible for Man not to create.

The Presence of
Unconditional Love
March 7, 2005

You should treat
your children as if
I, Lord Maitreya,
have come to you
as your child

Lord Maitreya
December 6, 2009

Lord Maitreya
December 6, 2009

I AM Maitreya.

I am so happy that I have this opportunity to come into your world again. I am happy like a child because it is my big dream to look into your world. I always wish to come. But the Cosmic Law does not allow me to do it, because your level of consciousness is not able to recognize me when I come.

You expect to see God the Almighty, but I am only a little child who possesses Great Wisdom.

Look at your children. The faces of many of them resemble the faces of great wise men. Look into their eyes. A newborn baby comes from our world. He remembers our world. And what does he see around him? He sees fuss. He sees a mess and a lot of noise. But he does not see that you wish to accept him as God, and that you want to know the secret that he came to tell the world.

In the first months of his life, a child is dwelling within our world half, or even most of the time. During this period, you have a lot to learn from him. Of course, he cannot teach you with words or actions, but he can convey to you the state of our world. This state is in his aura. And many people intuitively try to touch a child, pick him up in their arms, or pat him on his head. These automatic actions certainly allow you to come in touch with our world through the child.

But you have forgotten that your child is a messenger from our world; you indulge in your usual activities. You watch TV, talk on the phone, and listen to music. You wonder why your child is restless, why he often cries and is capricious.

But what you do differs so much from our world that a child is under continual stress. He cannot tell you to turn off the music or TV, and he cannot ask you to stop talking on the phone. He shows his displeasure with all this behavior by crying, and thereby shows you that he does not want all this commotion. But you think the child wants to eat, or drink, or he has just gotten tired and wants to sleep.

Your attitude toward your children needs to be reconsidered. You should treat your children as if I, Lord Maitreya, have come to you as your child.

Would you do in my presence all the things that you do in the presence of your child, thinking that he understands nothing?

Would you behave in the way that you behave?

I will come into incarnation, I do wish that, but I cannot do this until you change your attitude toward your children.

In the first months of life, a child's aura can be as large as a whole city. You truly meet the messenger of Heaven. But are you doing what is necessary to meet the messenger of Heaven?

You think that your children understand nothing.

You think they are silly and cannot perceive reality as you see it.

Children come into your world bearing the image of another world.

Many of them are wise souls who have passed the earth-school of initiations. And what do they see? They see parents and relatives using baby talk. And no one in the whole world treats them as wise souls who already know everything since their birth.

The aura of a baby gradually absorbs the environment of the family, the city, and the country in which he was born, and by the age of three, a child loses the memory of our world. He absorbs your habits, your attachments, and the stereotypes of your behavior. By the age of three, a child's aura is burdened with all the negative states that you have had and you still have. And if he watches TV or listens to the radio when you think he is asleep, or understanding nothing, then a child is imbued with the whole nightmare that flows like a river from your mass media. And who you see in front of you when he is three years old is already not an angel, having come into your world but a soul burdened with all the sins of the world, a soul who will have to work off the karma of the family, the karma of the kin, the karma of the country, and the karma of the world until the end of his earthly life.

I cannot come into your world until the world is ready to accept me. And if you think that the things that I am telling you are not true, that I am dramatizing or exaggerating, then you further postpone the time of my arrival in your world. As long as ignorance reigns in your world, as long as you perceive the simple truths as fairy tales, I will have nothing to do in your world.

I do aspire to come into embodiment as quickly as possible.

It is you, yourselves who can speed up my arrival.

You must have careful attitudes and not only to children. Every person living in the physical world has a right to be loved.

"Love thy neighbor as thyself," - it was so long ago that this commandment was given by beloved Jesus. So many events have taken place on Earth since the time of this commandment. How busy you are in your lives. You are constantly busy with something. Is it not the time to stop and hear Jesus' words addressed to you?

How many times is it necessary to repeat the commandments so that they are followed? How many times is it necessary to come with the Messages that you learn, not only to read or listen to them, but also to follow the received Teaching in your lives?

I will come again. I will give my Messages. And I do hope that there will be at least a hundred incarnated people on the globe who will not only read my Messages, but will also use them in life.

I AM Maitreya.

A Teaching on the liberation
from negative
energies

Kuthumi
December 12, 2009

Kuthumi
December 12, 2009

I AM Kuthumi.

Perhaps those of you who regularly read our Messages that we give through our Messenger will remember me. I come often, and my talks mainly concern the development of your consciousness. I also specialize in solving psychological problems with which your souls are burdened.

Today I would like to devote time to a talk about where your psychological problems come from and whether it is possible for you to free yourselves from them without the help of psychotherapists. It should be said that the Ascended Masters and human psychotherapists approach the liberation from psychological problems differently. Human psychotherapists use the terms "subconscious" and "unconscious," whereas I usually use the terms "soul" and "subtle bodies."

This would not be a big difference if your specialists approached you not as clients and sources of their subsistence in the physical world but as souls that need help and support.

I have to state the deplorable fact that practically all people living on planet Earth now are in need of help. And I mean help in solving psychological problems that are burdening their souls and pass from embodiment to embodiment. Many specialists and psychotherapists reject the fact that the soul has a very ancient history and passes through many incarnations. And this makes it impossible to fully help many souls who need help. Many problems came to them from their previous embodiments: various fears, phobias, and death records. Many souls are burdened with these problems and do not know how to free themselves from them.

I will not give you a universal prescription. I can only give you my own advice and recommendations. And I will be glad if you manage to use these recommendations in your lives. I will be even happier if my recommendations bring healing to your souls.

First, you need to realize that the problem is in you and burdens your subtle bodies. For example, this can be hatred toward the opposite sex, which originated from an experience in your past. In your current embodiment, you have a beautiful family and there is no cause for the manifestation of hatred and enmity. But you can do nothing with yourself. From time to time you experience attacks of hatred or anger. You suffer from this yourself, and it also affects the people close to you: your spouse and your children.

The first and most important step to solving your problem is the recognition of the fact that this problem exists within you. This is a very big and vital step. When you read these lines, it may seem funny to you that you cannot recognize such a problem. Do not jump to conclusions. You can see this problem in other people, but when the karmic energy of hatred and enmity rises within yourself, when it overwhelms you and totally flows over you like an ocean wave, you cannot evaluate the situation rationally. Your anger seems fully justified to you, and you find, or rather your carnal mind finds, a thousand satisfactory excuses for your state, your behavior, and your actions.

When this horrible, negative energy from your past embodiments rises within you, it is very difficult for you to cope with yourself. You do not know how many times in your past incarnations you experienced the most severe treatment from the opposite sex. You could have been humiliated, beaten up, and even violated and killed. The records of all these negative experiences are lying in your subtle bodies as a burden. And your task, your foremost task, is to try to realize that this energy, this negative energy, is present within you.

It is not your husband or wife that is the cause of your negative state of consciousness but the energy that exists within you. The complexity of the situation is that most likely within your husband or wife, there is also an energy that needs to be worked off. And, most probably, while under the influence of negative energy you blame your husband, for example, for some actions or thoughts that he does not have in the current embodiment; it was just in his previous embodiments he allowed himself to perform the precise actions you reproach him for. Therefore, the process of healing from low-quality energies becomes more complicated because this is a mutual process. You can render help to each other to free yourselves from the negative energies. You just need to agree between yourselves that when this negative energy is rising in one of you, the other must signal that here it is, this energy has risen. And then, helping each other, you will become aware of the presence of this energy within you. And you will be able to separate this energy from yourself.

You will become able to realize that this is the part of you that you wish to free yourself from.

The second vital step comes when you manage to recognize the presence of the negative energy that exists within you, and you begin to feel an impulse to get rid of that negative energy.

The next step is the easiest one. You ask God to liberate you from the negative energy that is present in you. But, with all its seeming simplicity, this step cannot be done by everybody. Usually, people are very mobile in their consciousness. They are able to ask God once or twice to free them from the negative energy, but then they forget about their appeal and about their decision to get rid of the negative energy. Then, when the next karmic moment comes and the negative energy totally overwhelms them again, people are puzzled. Why didn't God free them from this energy?

This, beloved, is because the negative energy that is present in you has sometimes been formed throughout the entire previous embodiment or during several embodiments. That is why you should go to great lengths to become free from this energy...

... Sometimes only your everyday endeavors during a number of years can help you to free yourself from the negative energies of the past.

The negative qualities that you acquired during the current embodiment are worked off much more easily, but the qualities that accompany you from embodiment to embodiment require a lot of effort to be worked off.

Many qualities can be worked off through the direct interaction with your spouses. Day after day, you face each other's negative qualities, and you realize that these are the negative energies that you need to free yourself from, and you forgive each other and help each other throughout your lives.

Only this way, by helping each other, are you sometimes able to overcome the karma of the past. And the main element that can help you in dissolving the past karma is the love that you feel toward each other. This is the greatest treasure of your world, which is worth cherishing and protecting much more than money, things, or gold.

I am glad that our talk has taken place today.

I AM Kuthumi,
with Love to you and your souls.

Every person living in the physical world has a right to be loved.

"Love thy neighbor as thyself," - it was so long ago that this commandment was given by beloved Jesus.

So many events have taken place on Earth since the time of this commandment. How busy you are in your lives. You are constantly busy with something. Is it not the time to stop and hear Jesus' words addressed to you?

Lord Maitreya
December 6, 2009

A Teaching
on the correct use
of sexual energy

Serapis Bey
December 15, 2009

Serapis Bey
December 15, 2009

I AM Serapis Bey. You know me, as I often come through this Messenger.

You may also know that I serve on the ray of the lowest chakra, the Muladhara.

Your Kundalini energy is dormant in this chakra. At the time of your Ascension into the Light, an intense white light comes out of this chakra and the Divine energy literally lifts you off the physical plane, and raises you up into the Higher octaves.

That is why I am the Master who teaches disciples on the Path how to treat the energy of the Divine Mother in the correct way.

I am aware that the morals of humanity have degenerated greatly over the last several hundred years.

This concerns the attitude toward sexual energy as well.

Today I have to give a Teaching that will make many of you take another look at your sexual desires. And the purpose of my instruction is to protect those souls who are able to hear me from falling lower by misusing their sexual energy.

What new things can I say and how can I instruct you on what was already known to humankind many hundreds and thousands of years ago? Your culture ignores many things that are so natural and have been passed on from generation to generation, for thousands of years. This is a Teaching on the correct use of sexual energy. It is exactly your attitude toward your inner power, your sexual potential that determines your further evolutionary path.

When you are able to use your sexual energy intelligently, you overcome the animal part of yourself and approach becoming a Divine human. The subject of my talk may appall many of you, because your actions in the past were not so perfect. Every time you thoughtlessly and unnecessarily waste your Divine potential, you create karma. Your creative power, your creative ability, and your health depend directly on your ability to control your sexual energy.

Society does not provide an adequate explanation of this subject in school, or in the education of future parents. However, this important subject must occupy your mind, and when you begin to think about this topic, there is the possibility that you will be able to properly control your sexual energy in future.

As I mentioned, sexual energy is directly related to your creative power, the ability to create in any sphere of human activity.

Your sexual energy is used as fuel during your Ascension. Hence, the conclusion is that a careful, extremely careful attitude toward this type of energy is required.

You may not agree with me and state the fact that the energy is given by God, and so the source of this energy is unlimited.

This is true, but only on the condition that you have mastered the right attitude toward this type of energy. Why do you think so many miracles of materialization, teleportation, and others are impossible in your time? One reason is that the flow of Divine energy into your body is closed to a great degree. You do not have access to the Divine energy even to the extent that was possible just a few thousand years ago. The flow of Divine energy is being restricted even more as humanity increasingly falls into ignorance.

You think ignorance means that you cannot use a TV, a computer, or a cell phone. No, ignorance is that you do not follow the Divine Law that exists in this Universe. And one of the points of this Law states the need to carefully use our sexual energy.

Each person possesses a certain potential. And this potential can be depleted prematurely. In such a case, you will not be able to fulfill your Divine plan and your Divine mission, and you will become a hollow person, a person without God within himself or herself. Your eyes are dying, so you become the living dead, even in the course of your earthly life.

Sexual culture is part of the general culture of society. What we witness now is the stage of dissolution of morals in society as it was in the days of Sodom and Gomorrah. You may have heard what happened to these cities.

All people are at different stages of evolutionary development. There are a very small percentage of people who are capable of using the Divine energy in the right way since their birth. These are the virgins of Sanat Kumara.

In essence, these people are very great incarnations, or they are partial incarnations. Other people are able to control their sexual energy and keep it within certain bounds. But for this they must be aware of what the consequences are for the unnecessary waste of sexual energy. All the stereotypes of behavior in your society and mass culture are not conducive to the creation of the right patterns in this field. Therefore, it is necessary to have internal and conscious resistance to your temptations.

In any case, this precious energy must not be used for pleasure. It would be perfect to use this energy only for conceiving children.

I have talked about two categories of people who can fully or partially control their sexual energy. Unfortunately, the rest of the people have fallen even lower than animals in this matter, because what is allowed in mass media and on the Internet cannot be described by any other words but absolute dissolution of morals.

The lightest energy that makes you similar to Gods has been associated in the minds of humanity with debauchery and something unclean.

Your minds must be put in order. You must separate the Divine from what is evil regarding this subject. You must separate the wheat from the chaff in this matter, primarily because the greatest distortion of the Divine energy in the world is connected exactly with all kinds of sexual distortions.

I am glad that I have managed to conduct a talk on this important topic. And I will be even happier if there are a sufficient number of individuals among those people who will read this talk of mine and who will manifest firmness and persistence, and will find the strength to restrain their desires and raise their Kundalini energy as a sign of their devotion to the Will of God.

I AM Serapis Bey.

At the beginning of Creation, God divided his Love into an infinite number of parts, and each of you, being a part of God, received your own little part of Love.

Beloved Surya
July 4, 2006

You can
start your service
exactly where you
are at this moment

Beloved Nada
December 17, 2009

Beloved Nada
December 17, 2009

I AM Nada... My task for today is to give you an idea of the role that each of you can play in your lives.

There are certain expectations in your mind concerning your possible service to the Brotherhood. I must clarify this point for you. Beloved, you do not need to wait until you obtain opportunities, money, power or position.

When you think you need something, in addition to what you already have to start your service, you act according to the prompting of your carnal mind. The only thing you need to start your service to the Brotherhood is your desire. Nothing else is needed.

You can start your service exactly where you are at this moment. Everything you are doing now can be directed by you for the service to the Brotherhood. Look, what are you doing now?

You are at home and you are busy with your household duties. It's beautiful! You are already serving the Brotherhood!

How can it be that when you clean the house or wash the dishes you are also serving the Brotherhood? Oh beloved, the point is in the way you are doing it. Even the smallest and most insignificant task that you do in your life can be done with great Love. If you perform small deeds with great Love, thinking about how your family and your closest ones will be happy when they enter a clean home and put on their snow-white and freshly laundered clothes, then you are already serving the Brotherhood. Your service can be manifested in every task. And if you do your work very carefully and with Love, any one of your activities will transform the space there. And when your children or spouse comes home tired and burdened from the bustle that they have been in all day, the atmosphere of Love that you have created at home can transform their hearts and restore harmony in their souls.

It is very difficult to maintain inner balance and feelings of Love when you are at work, because not all of the people you encounter during the day are harmonious and friendly. You more often face imperfect manifestations of human consciousness. And that is where a wide field for your action opens for you, for your service. You must master the skill of neutralizing any negativity using Love, patience, and humility. You are given so many opportunities in your life to manifest your service! Almost every task, every meeting, everything that happens to you during the day can be used to fulfill your service. Because only when you learn to find the points in your life where you can apply the best qualities of your soul in everyday activities and in the details of life, and only when none of the outer problems can break your inner peace and harmony, only then will the other opportunity for your service appear. And you will be able to use the qualities that you have already developed in the new stage of your service to the Brotherhood, which is inseparable from service to Life.

Many of you seek the help of the Ascended Masters and ask to be given an opportunity to serve, to be given an opportunity to prove yourself in service. Beloved, be honest with yourself. God has already taken care of everything. You already have the best conditions to start your service, and to work on those qualities of yours that prevent you from manifesting Love and care for your neighbors in the most difficult life situations. Until you learn to see great service in the little nothings of life, you will not be able to progress along the Path, because many of you wish to become Messengers, or manage our organizations. Look, what do you really want? Do you want to be somebody or to manage something, or do you really wish to serve?

The answer to this question will determine your future life. You will either struggle to the end of your life to take up a post or to prove to someone that you already have great spiritual attainments, or you will serve without attracting any outside attention and do God's deeds on Earth, and subsequently, on a much larger scale.

I have come to you today in order to give you an understanding of true service and false service. Yes, beloved, since everything in your world has two sides, likewise service has two different sides.

Always, before you start doing something, think about what you are really driven by. Is it a desire to prove something to others, to show your greatness and to show everyone your diligence? Or are you driven by

Love for your neighbor, a Love that is inherent in you and affects everything you do? Very simple things that you perform selflessly, with great unconditional Love remain with you forever as the treasures of your causal body. Your current earthly life will be over, but your attitude toward deeds and toward people will remain, and will accompany you in your next incarnation.

Your world lacks so much for this quality of true service to Life, which is automatically the service to the Brotherhood, because the main goal of the Great White Brotherhood is service to humankind of Earth.

I have told you simple truths today. I am even convinced that you already know all of this, or you have read it or heard of it.

Yet, let me ask you: What prevents you from applying this knowledge in your lives?

There is sometimes an abyss between something that you know, or have read or heard of and your real application of this knowledge in your lives.

You need to think more about what prevents you from manifesting Divine qualities in your life and gradually, step by step, get rid of everything that impedes you.

I would not have become the Ascended Lady Master if I had not mastered all of this science that I teach you, in practice, in my incarnations. I have gone through the earthly school, and now I have an opportunity to be of greater service to humankind.

Do not think that your attitude toward work, people, plants, or animals goes unnoticed if there are no witnesses to your good deeds or actions. Everything is recorded in the Akashic Records: your every action, thought, feeling, and deed, both negative and positive. Think about it, and go through your life carefully, leaving behind no astral or mental garbage.

May all your progress through life be accompanied only by Love and the fragrance of roses!

With Love, I AM Nada.

True Love begins with the veneration of a woman, a Mother. The feelings you experience towards your Mother can leave their mark on your whole life.

The Presence of
Unconditional Love
March 7, 2005

**You create your
future and the future
of the whole planet**
at the moment of
conception of your
child

*Kuthumi
June 17, 2011*

Kuthumi
June 17, 2011

I AM Kuthumi, having come to you to give
a discourse that will be useful for your souls.

Today we are going to talk about the concerns that are very close and understandable to everyone. More specifically, we are going to talk about your future — about your children, and about the generation of people that will replace you.

By human standards a short period of time will pass, and a new generation of people will replace the generation that is living now. And each successive generation should be better than the previous one. However, this does not always happen. Why? Perhaps many of you wondered why your children are different from you. Why are they impudent, disobedient, and guided in their lives by completely different principles from those you were guided by in your time? What is the reason for this?

I will approach this subject from a standpoint that is probably unexpected for you. I will ask you to remember the period of time that preceded the moment when your child was born. There is no need to share this memory with anyone. Just try to recollect how it happened that a baby was born to you.

Perhaps you will remember that you accidentally discovered that you will have a baby. You might have even been sad or vexed by that fact. Maybe you had not even planned to have a baby and yet he emerged.

What were you thinking about when enjoying a love affair with your partner? I suppose that most of you were not thinking about creating a new human being who was to come to this world and become a creator of this world.

Your energy flows where your attention is directed. You were thinking about getting pleasure for yourself or for your sex partner, weren't you? Thus, the precious Divine energy was directed at getting pleasure.

But the Divine Will played a trick on you and a baby appeared. What did your child get in this case? What part of the Divine energy?

You yourself disposed of the Divine energy and directed it to getting pleasure. What, from that precious energy, did a new being who was so eager to get into your world receive?

You supplied your child with only the residual amount of the Divine energy. That is, the entire Divine energy boost that was supposed to accompany your child throughout all his life remained on the things around you when you were seeking pleasures.

I think now you remember that moment.

Some of you may say that you were expecting a baby and praying for his or her birth. And indeed, your child was long expected and welcomed by you. But remember those days of your youth that preceded your child's birth.

You wanted to get sexual pleasure, and you experimented with your sexual energy. You did many things that you are even ashamed to remember. And every time you got pleasure you wasted your sexual potential, which was required for your child's birth so that your child would be healthy not only physically but also mentally. And when you settled down and were looking forward to the conception of your long-awaited first-born child, do you think that he received much of the Divine energy? Didn't you supply your child only with the residual amount?

If your sexual pleasures were wild and indecent, what soul do you think you can attract as your child? Everything is attracted according to vibrations. And, the soul you will attract as your first-born child will be attracted to you after you have burdened yourself with a significant amount of karma accumulated while satisfying your desires.

After your reflection, have you come to realize that you yourselves are to blame for all the problems of the next generation of people on planet Earth?

You cannot say that you have nothing to do with the fact that every new generation is less and less viable than the previous one.

Therefore, in order to change the situation on the planet, we come and give our Teaching. You should be clearly aware of the connection between your actions and the consequences of your actions.

Only when you learn to control your desires, thoughts, and feelings, will you be able to gradually overcome the karma of your past wrong choices and deeds.

However, I must warn you about another mistake. Many of you are inclined to blame yourselves for those improper deeds that you performed in your youth. And sometimes this feeling of guilt gives rise to a whole range of psychological problems. And instead of strengthening your focus on your child and family in order to correct your past mistakes, you plunge into depression and even start to feel fear of Divine punishment.

Beloved, God does not want to punish you. He wants you to realize your mistakes and not to repeat them in the future. There is no sinner without a future. And sometimes a person who has realized his mistakes and repented for them can do much more for humankind than a person who does not commit any improper acts because of fear of Divine punishment.

Direct your energy to a positive path! Do not chew over the scenes of your past sins and mistakes again and again. That will only make matters worse because you will be directing energy to the same wrong path. The river of the Divine energy that flows through you should find a new channel and wash away the consequences of all the past wrong states of consciousness.

Constantly concentrating on the positive and on a desire to help those around you, especially your children, can transform the energy of past mistakes and create a new opportunity for the future of your children.

Complete realization of past mistakes and a fervent desire not to repeat them are quite enough to change the karmic consequences and create a bright future for your children.

Do not forget that you have created karmic connections with your children. And there is a strong probability that in your future incarnations you will be the children of those individuals who are your children now. In order to alleviate your karma in the future, you should primarily be concerned about the souls of your children now.

Everything in the world is interconnected, and you need to be very careful and thoughtful about everything that you do.

The purpose of my talk today was to give you the knowledge about the importance of a thoughtful approach to planning a child's birth. In fact, you create your own future and the future of the whole planet at the moment of conception of your child. Think about that the next time you satisfy your sexual desire.

I AM Kuthumi,
with care for your souls and the souls
of all living beings.

You can start your service exactly where you are at this moment.

...Even the smallest and most insignificant task that you do in your life can be done with great Love.

Beloved Nada
December 17, 2009

I do not know why God chose me to give the Teaching in the form of Messages from Heaven. This Teaching covers all spheres of human life.

During the period from March 4, 2005 to June 20, 2018, I received more than 480 Messages. During this time, more than thirty books have been published.

It would be good if this work found its reader, for whom it is intended and who is in need of it, as a drink of pure water for the thirsty.

Tatyana Mickushina

T. Mickushina's official websites
http://sirius-eng.net/
http://sirius-ru.net/

Words of Wisdom Series of Books

The books contain Messages given by the Ascended Masters through their Messenger Tatyana N Mickushina from 2005 through 2017. During this time the people of Earth have been given the Teaching of the True purpose of evolution the aspiration of every soul to the Creator, to union with God, and adherence to the Highest Moral Law that exists in the Universe. This harmonious Unified Teaching also contains Teachings about the distinction between Good and Evil, the Path of Initiation, the change of consciousness, about Love, Karma, Freedom, happiness, nonviolence, about the Community, and many other Teachings.

Tatyana N. Mickushina

IF YOU LOVE, IT MEANS YOU ARE ALIVE!

Please, leave your review about this book at amazon.com. This will greatly help in spreading the Teaching of the Ascended Masters given through the Messenger Tatyana Mickushina.

Websites:
http://sirius-eng.net (English version)
http://sirius-ru.net (Russian version)

Books by T.N.Mickushina on amazon.com:
amazon.com/author/tatyana_mickushina

Made in the USA
San Bernardino, CA
01 June 2020

72605667R00071